Weather Watchers

Thunder and Lightning

Cassie Mayer

www.heinemann.co.uk/library
Visit our website to find out more information about Heinemann Library books.

To order:
 Phone 44 (0) 1865 888066
Send a fax to 44 (0) 1865 314091
Visit the Heinemann Bookshop at www.heinemann.co.uk/library to browse our
 catalogue and order online.

First published in Great Britain by Heinemann Library,
Halley Court, Jordan Hill, Oxford OX2 8EJ, part of Harcourt
Education. Heinemann is a registered trademark of Harcourt
Education Ltd.

© Harcourt Education Ltd 2007
First published in paperback in 2007
The moral right of the proprietor has been asserted.

Editorial: Tracey Crawford, Cassie Mayer, Dan Nunn,
and Sarah Chappelow
Design: Jo Hinton-Malivoire
Picture Research: Tracy Cummins, Tracey Engel,
and Ruth Blair
Production: Duncan Gilbert

Originated by Chroma Graphics (Overseas) Pte. Ltd
Printed and bound in China by South China
Printing Company

ISBN 978 0 431 18255 1 (hardback)
11 10 09 08 07
10 9 8 7 6 5 4 3 2 1

ISBN 978 0 431 18372 5 (paperback)
12 11 10 09 08
10 9 8 7 6 5 4 3 2 1

British Library Cataloguing in Publication Data
Mayer, Cassie
Thunder and lightning. - (Weather watchers)
1.Thunder - Juvenile literature 2.Lightning - Juvenile
literature 3.Thunderstorms - Juvenile literature
I.Title
551.5'54

Acknowledgements
The publishers would like to thank the following for permission
to reproduce photographs: Corbis pp. 4 (cloud; sunshine, G.
Schuster/zefa; rain, Anthony Redpath), 7 (Bill Ross), 8 (Jim Reed),
14 (A & J Verkaik), 16 (Layne Kennedy), 19 (Craig Aurness),
20 (John Lund); Getty Images pp. 4 (snow, Marc Wilson
Photography), 5, 6 (Vince Streano), 9 (Joe Drivas), 10 (Jim Reed),
11 (Eddie Soloway), 12 (Chad Ehlers), 13 (Kenneth Garrett), 15
(David R. Frazier), 17 (Richard Kaylin), 18, 21 (Michael K. Nichols),
23 (lightning, Vince Streano; thunder cloud, Jim Reed).

Cover photograph reproduced with permission of Corbis (Aaron
Horowitz). Back cover photograph reproduced with permission of
Getty Images.

Every effort has been made to contact copyright holders of any
material reproduced in this book. Any omissions will be rectified in
subsequent printings if notice is given to the publishers.

Contents

What is weather?

There are many types of weather.
Weather changes all the time.

Thunder and lightning
are types of weather.

What is lightning?

Lightning is a flash of light
in the sky during a storm.

Lightning comes from a cloud.

Lightning can strike land.

Lightning can strike water.

What is thunder?

Thunder is the sound of lightning.

You cannot see thunder, but you can hear it. It is loud when lightning is nearby.

Lightning can happen when it is warm.

Lightning can happen when it rains.

Types of lightning

Some lightning stays in a cloud.

Some lightning strikes the ground.

Some lightning strikes one place.

Some lightning strikes many places at once.

Keeping safe

Lightning can be dangerous.

Stay inside when there is lightning.

Thunder and lightning can be exciting.

Thunder and lightning show us the power of weather.

What to do in a thunderstorm

If you are inside:
• Stay away from windows
• Do not use the phone

If you are outside:
• Try to find safe shelter
• Do not stand near a tree
• Stay away from water
• Crouch down and hug your knees

Picture glossary

 lightning a flash of light in the sky. Lightning comes from a cloud.

 thunder the sound that lightning makes. You hear thunder after you see lightning.

Index

Notes to parents and teachers
Before reading
Talk about different weather. Ask the children which type of weather they like best. Have they ever been out in a storm? Was it exciting?

After reading
Sing the nursery rhyme: "I hear thunder" with hand actions.
Create a stormy picture on black paper with rough sea at the bottom and forked lightning striking down from grey clouds.
Play the thunder and lightning game: Divide the children into teams. Place 6 beanbags in a zigzag pattern on the hall floor. Each team member should take it in turns to be forked lightning and run down the zigzag pattern. When all team members get to the end they should drum their feet on the floor to represent thunder. The first team to finish is the winner.